The Panama Canal: 66 Fascinating Facts For Kids

Peter Nielsen

All rights reserved. No part of this publication may be reproduced in any form or by any means, including scanning, photocopying, or otherwise, without prior written permission of the copyright holder. Copyright Peter Nielsen © 2020

This book is just one of a series of "Fascinating Facts For Kids" books. For more fascinating facts about people, history, animals, and much more, please visit:

www.fascinatingfactsforkids.com

Contents

The Search for a Shortcut............ 1

The French Attempt......................5

The United States Takes Over...... 10

Work Begins.................................. 13

The Plan.. 17

The Culebra Cut............................ 20

The Gatun Dam & Lake..................22

The Locks..25

Completion.................................... 29

Assorted Panama Canal Facts...... 33

Illustration Attributions...............36

The Search for a Shortcut

1. When 16th-century European explorers wanted to sail from the Atlantic Ocean to the Pacific Ocean, the huge continents of North and South America stood in their way. They had to travel thousands of miles to sail round the southern tip of South America, passing through some of the most dangerous waters in the world.

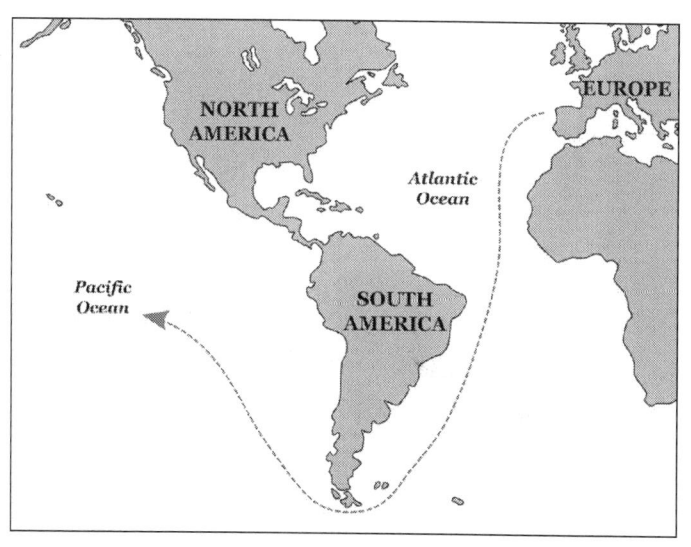

2. Just to the north of the South American continent, in present-day Panama, is a narrow strip of land which separates the Atlantic and Pacific Oceans. If the European explorers could find a way to somehow get their ships across this strip of land (called an "isthmus"), their journey to the Pacific would be much shorter and less dangerous.

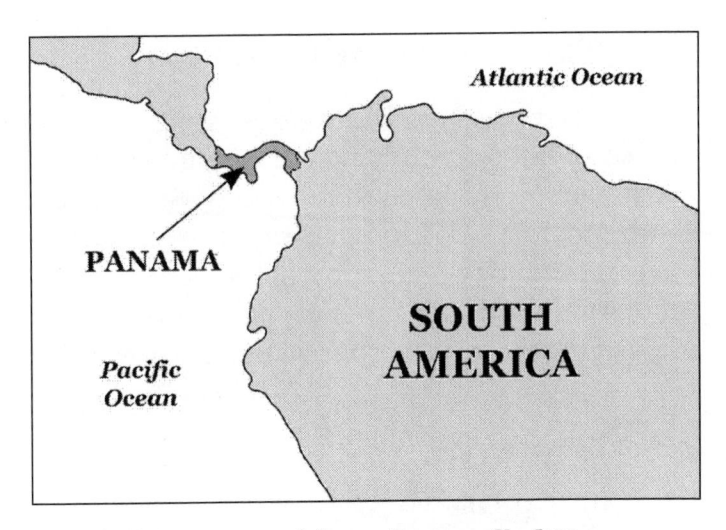

3. In 1513, a Spanish explorer called Vasco Nunez de Balboa led the first expedition across the isthmus. He and his men hacked their way for fifty miles (80 km) through some of the thickest and most mountainous jungle in the world, before reaching the Pacific Ocean nearly one month later and claiming the isthmus for the Spanish king.

Vasco Nunez de Balboa

4. De Balboa and other Spanish explorers who followed him could find no waterway that linked the two oceans, so it was decided to try to dig a canal across the isthmus. But it became obvious that the thick, swampy jungle would make it impossible to build a canal, and Spanish interest in the project ended.

5. It wasn't until the early nineteenth century that interest in the building of a canal across Panama was revived. Many countries made plans, and the United States even built a railroad across the isthmus, but it was French who would lead the way in the construction of a canal.

The French Attempt

6. In 1859, the French had begun work on an ambitious project to construct a 100-mile-long (160 km) canal, the Suez Canal, which would link the Mediterranean Sea with the Red Sea. Ten years later the canal was finished, and ships could travel from Europe to Asia without having to sail for thousands of miles round the continent of Africa.

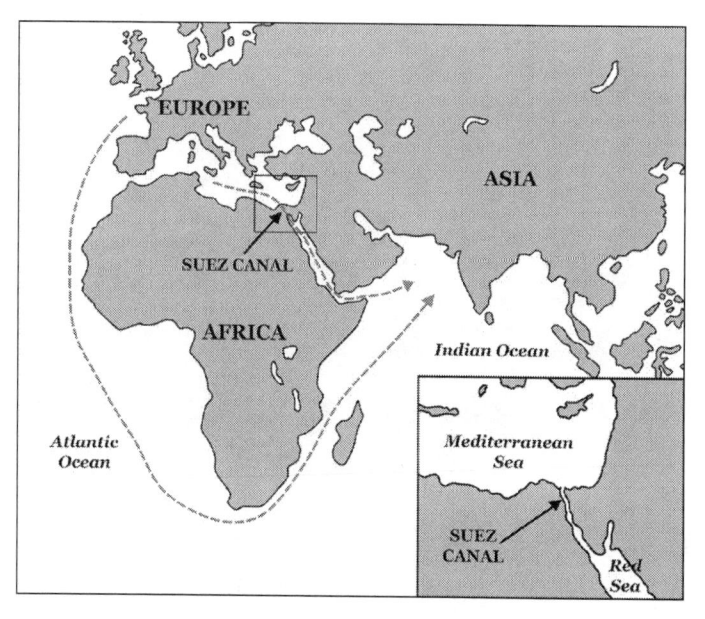

7. The man who had been in charge of the Suez Canal project was Ferdinand de Lesseps, and in 1875 he was chosen to oversee the building of a canal across the Isthmus of Panama.

Ferdinand de Lesseps

8. The building of the Suez Canal had been a monumental achievement and had made de Lesseps a hero in France, but building a canal through Panama would be much more difficult. The Suez Canal had been dug over ground that was at sea level and ran through empty desert, but Panama was covered in thick jungle and it poured with rain for more than half the year. There was also a mountain range to get through.

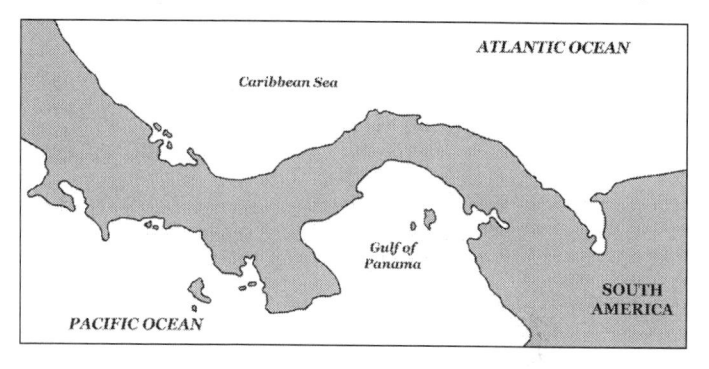

The Isthmus of Panama

9. De Lesseps had two options to choose from to get his canal across the mountains of Panama. He could dig a channel deep down into the rock so that the canal could be at sea level for its whole length. Or he could build a series of locks, which would be like a huge water-filled staircase, to transport ships over the mountains.

10. De Lesseps had had great success with his sea level canal at Suez, and he thought that building a series of locks would be too complicated. Against the advice of his engineers, de Lesseps decided to build a sea level canal through Panama.

11. De Lesseps hired thousands of men to do the back-breaking work of digging the canal; using shovels, picks, and wheelbarrows. Work began in 1881, but it soon became obvious that de Lesseps would face many problems and obstacles.

12. The construction of the canal started during Panama's rainy season, which lasts from May to November. The constant rain caused machinery to rust in just a few days, and the heavy water-logged ground became impossible to dig out.

13. The mighty Chagres River flows rapidly down from the mountains of Panama and its banks would often burst, causing mudslides and flooding that would fill in any digging that had been done.

14. The humid, swampy jungle of Panama was home to many dangerous animals, including poisonous snakes and deadly big cats such as cougars and jaguars. But perhaps the most dangerous threat came from mosquitoes which spread the deadly diseases of malaria and yellow fever.

A mosquito on human skin

15. In the late nineteenth century, the causes of malaria and yellow fever were not understood – we now know that the diseases are spread by mosquito bites – and so any health measures that were put in place were ineffective. It is thought that around 20,000 men died from the diseases during the time of the French attempt to build the Panama Canal.

16. Ferdinand de Lesseps and his thousands of men battled against the odds for eight years in the sweltering heat of the Panama jungle. But no solution was found to deal with the Chagres River, and in May 1889 the French finally admitted defeat and abandoned the Panama Canal project.

17. Although the French had stopped work in Panama, they still held the legal rights to build a canal there. They had lost a lot of money in their failed attempt and hoped to get some of it back by selling the rights to another country. That country would be the United States of America.

The United States Takes Over

18. In September 1901, Theodore Roosevelt became president of the United States and he was keen for America to build a canal linking the Atlantic and Pacific Oceans. But the French failure made him think that Panama was a bad choice and decided that the best place to build a canal was across the Central American country of Nicaragua.

19. When the French heard of the American plan, they offered them the rights to build the Panama Canal for $100 million. The United States, knowing that they were the only interested buyers, offered just $40 million, which the French rejected. The United States went ahead with their plan for a canal in Nicaragua and the French, fearing they were risking getting no money at all, decided to accept the American offer of $40 million.

20. At the beginning of the twentieth century, Panama was part of the South American country of Colombia, and although the Americans had bought the rights from the French, they would still need the agreement of the Colombian government to build the canal.

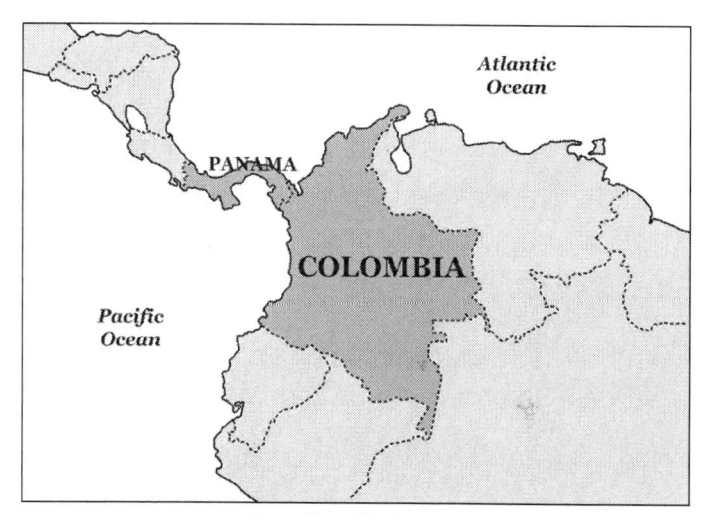

21. The Americans drew up an agreement, but the Colombians were not happy with it and refused permission for the Americans to build the canal. The people of Panama were unhappy, as they wanted the project to go ahead, and they decided to take matters into their own hands.

22. For a long time, Panama had wanted to separate from Colombia, and the Panama Canal project gave them the chance to become an independent country. They had the powerful United States on their side, and on November 3, 1903, Panama started a rebellion against Colombia to fight for its independence.

23. The Colombian government sent soldiers to put down the rebellion, but the United States had sent warships to Panama in support of the Panamanian people. The sight of the United States Navy off the coast of Panama eventually caused the Colombians to turn round and head home. Panama had achieved its independence with hardly a shot being fired.

24. The United States drew up an agreement with Panama to build the canal. America was given control of a strip of land ten miles (16 km) wide, called the "Canal Zone," where the canal would be built. In return, the United States would pay Panama $10 million followed by annual payments of $250,000. The United States could now finish the work the French had started more than twenty years ago.

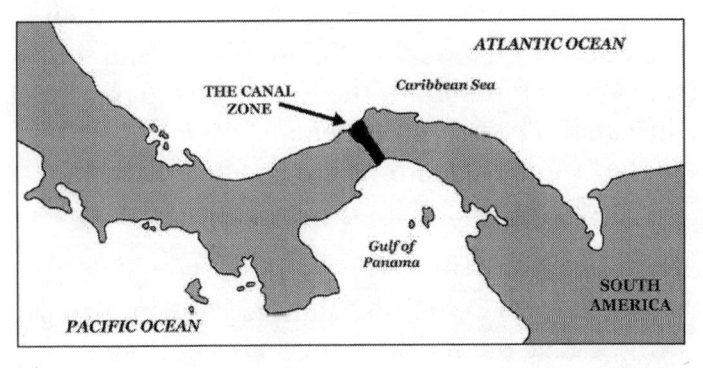

Work Begins

25. In June 1904, President Roosevelt appointed John F. Wallace, a respected railroad engineer, as chief engineer for the Panama Canal project. He was paid a yearly salary of $25,000, making him the highest-paid government employee apart from the president.

26. When the French withdrew from Panama in 1889, they left behind buildings, machinery, and other equipment that the Americans intended to use. But when Wallace arrived in Panama he found buildings that were falling apart and rusty machinery covered by undergrowth.

27. The thousands of men who went to Panama to work on the canal had been promised a decent environment in which to live and work, but they were forced to live in overcrowded and filthy conditions. The food they were given often made them ill, and there was the constant danger of catching malaria or yellow fever. Morale was very low and many men left Panama as soon as they could.

28. Life was difficult during the first year in Panama, but things changed when Wallace resigned as chief engineer in June 1905. President Roosevelt replaced him with John Frank Stevens, who had spent his life building railroads across North America.

John Frank Stevens

29. When Stevens arrived in Panama he saw the appalling conditions that his workers had to endure. He set about improving things by ordering the construction of new, clean houses for his men to live in. To solve the food problem he built shops that sold food sent from the United States.

30. Stevens also encouraged his men to bring their wives and children to Panama so that families could be together. Schools, hospitals, and sports clubs were built, and soon whole communities were established that were pleasant places to live. For many, the standard of living in Panama was better than they had in the United States.

31. To solve the problem of malaria and yellow fever, President Roosevelt sent an expert in tropical disease, William Gorgas, to Panama. Gorgas knew that malaria and yellow fever were spread by mosquitoes, and he had an ambitious plan to rid the Canal Zone of the disease-carrying insects.

William Gorgas

32. Gorgas got his men to fumigate every building in the Canal Zone and put up screens in all the windows. Water is a breeding ground for mosquitoes, so kerosene was poured on every puddle, pond, and swamp to kill the mosquitoes and their eggs.

33. Ridding the Canal Zone of mosquitoes was time-consuming and expensive. It took eighteen months before the area was free of mosquitoes, but in the end it was successful, with the last case of yellow fever being reported in December 1905.

The Plan

34. When the improvement in living conditions had been competed, work resumed on the building of the canal. The original plan had been to follow the French idea of a sea level canal, but after two years of discussion it was decided that a canal with locks would be built.

35. Although building a lock canal was more complicated, it would need much less digging than a sea level canal, and would take around half the time to complete. The canal would be constructed in a series of three major projects:

- Digging a nine-mile-long (14 km) channel, known as the "Culebra Cut," through the mountains.
- Building a dam across the Chagres River.
- Building six enormous double locks.

36. When ships from the Pacific Ocean entered the canal a series of locks would lift them eighty-five feet (26 m) above sea level. After leaving the highest of the locks they would sail north along the Culebra Cut.

37. After sailing the length of the Culebra Cut ships would enter a huge man-made lake – Gatun Lake – created by building a dam across the Chagres River, causing the surrounding land to flood.

38. Ships would sail across Gatun Lake to another series of locks which would take them down to sea level again, where the canal would take them out into the Atlantic Ocean. The whole process would be over in a matter of hours, instead of the weeks it would take to sail round the South American continent.

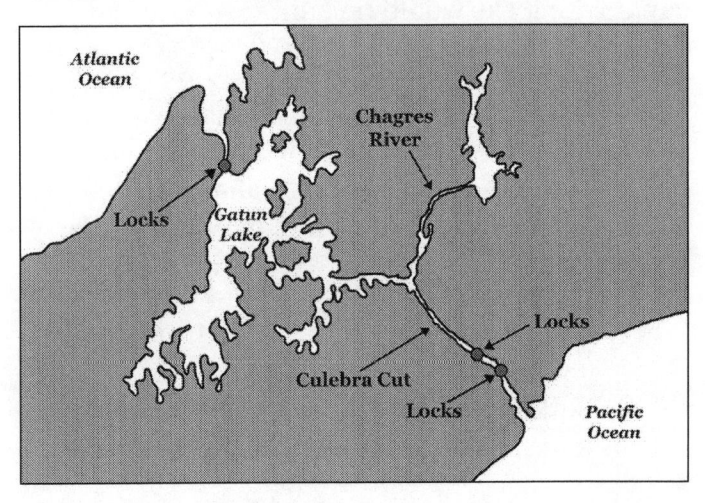

39. John Frank Stevens unexpectedly resigned as chief engineer in January 1907, and would not see work on the Panama Canal completed. President Roosevelt was furious that he had lost another chief engineer, and he replaced Stevens with Colonel George Washington Goethals, a military man who would never desert his post.

George Washington Goethals

The Culebra Cut

40. Stevens had already made good progress on the construction of the canal, and Goethals did not try to change too much. But there was a lot of work still to be done, especially on the most challenging part of the canal – the Culebra Cut.

41. The Culebra Cut was a huge channel dug out of the Cordillera Mountains. Some of the digging was done with picks and shovels, but most was done using huge digging machines and dynamite.

Working on the Culebra Cut in 1907

42. The use of dynamite meant that huge amounts of rock could be blasted out of the mountains quickly. But dynamite was dangerous to work with, often exploding unexpectedly for no apparent reason. Many men were killed or lost limbs during the construction of the Culebra Cut.

43. Huge ships would use the canal when it was finished, so vast amounts of earth and rock had to be dug away. The finished Culebra Cut would be nine miles (14 km) long, 150 feet (45 m) deep, and 300 feet (90 m) wide.

44. Landslides were a huge problem at the Culebra Cut, especially during the rainy season. Huge amounts of mud and rock would slide down the mountain sides before filling the cut and burying machinery. Weeks of work could be wasted by a single landslide, and digging would have to be started all over again.

45. Newspaper reports about the Panama Canal project fascinated people back in the United States, and the digging of the Culebra Cut created the most interest. It soon became a popular tourist attraction with up to 20,000 Americans a year traveling to Panama. People would stand on a mountain ridge above the Culebra Cut to watch the work going on beneath them.

The Gatun Dam & Lake

46. The main obstacle that had defeated the French was the wild, fast-flowing Chagres River which stood in the path of the canal's route. But the Americans had a plan – they would build a dam. It would be built near the village of Gatun and be called the Gatun Dam.

47. Building a dam across the Chagres River would cause water to spread for miles over the surrounding countryside, creating a huge, calm lake. When finished, it would spread for 164 square miles (425 sq km) over land that had once been jungle, making it the largest man-made lake ever built at the time.

48. As well as controlling the flow of the Chagres River, the new lake - called Gatun Lake – would become part of the Panama Canal. Ships would leave the Culebra Cut and sail for more than twenty miles (32 km) across the lake before joining the rest of the canal. Creating the lake needed no digging, and a tremendous amount of time and money was saved.

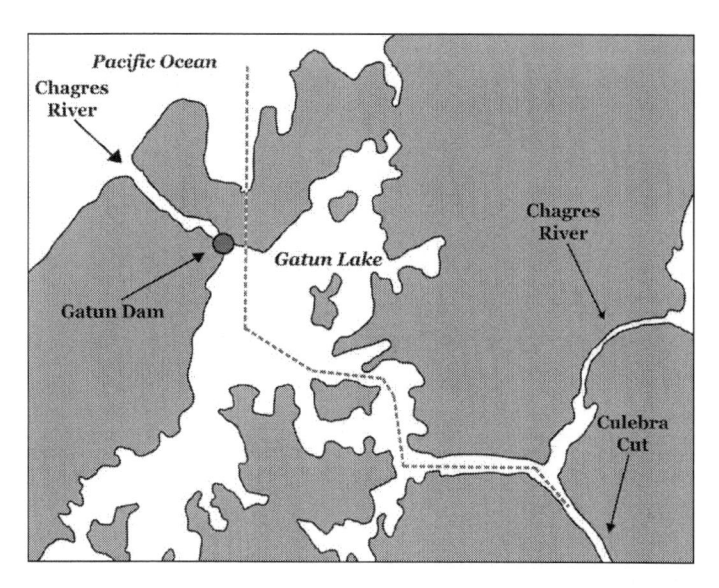

49. The Gatun Dam was built across a narrow river valley using rock and earth that had been dug out of the Culebra Cut and brought to the dam by train. Rock was used to build two parallel walls across the river, and a mixture of earth, sand, and mud was pumped into the space between the walls. As it dried out the mixture became as hard as cement and strong enough to control the flow of the mighty Chagres River.

50. It took six years to build the Gatun Dam and when it was finished it stretched for one and a half miles (2.4 km) across the river valley. It was half a mile (0.8 km) wide at its base and more than 100 feet high, and at the time it was the largest dam in the world to be built using earth.

The finished Gatun Dam

The Locks

51.   Six locks would be built, three at the Pacific end of the canal, and another three at the Atlantic end. The locks on the Pacific end would gradually lift ships from sea level up to the Culebra Cut, eighty-five feet (26 m) higher. The Atlantic locks would raise ships up to the entrance of Gatun Lake. Each of the locks had two chambers so that ships in one chamber could move up while ships in the other chamber were moving down.

52.   When a ship enters a lock, the gates behind it close to form a water-tight chamber. Water is pumped into the chamber, raising the ship to the next level. The gate in front of the ship is then opened and the ship sails to the next lock. When all three locks of the Panama Canal had been passed through, ships would sail into Gatun Lake or the Culebra Cut where they would continue their journey to locks on the other side of Panama which would lower them back to sea level.

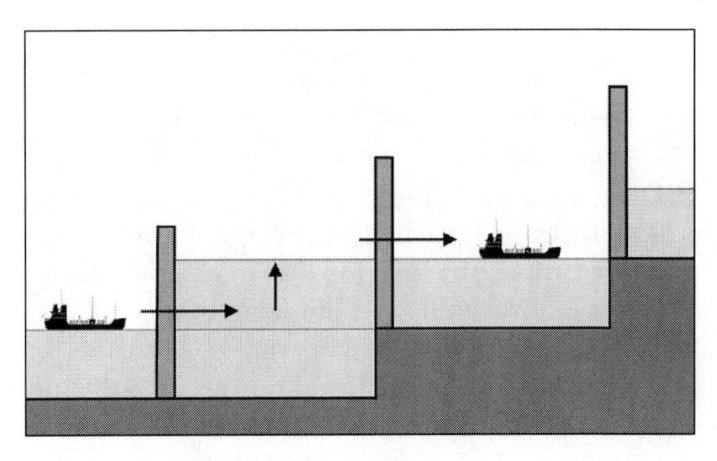

How a lock works

53. The locks of the Panama Canal would have to hold some of the biggest ships in the world, and they would be the largest locks ever built. Each chamber had walls and a floor of thick concrete and was eighty feet (25 m) deep, 110 feet (33 m) wide, and 1,000 feet (76 m) long - only 250 feet (76 m) shorter than the height of the Empire State Building.

The locks under construction in 1910

54. At the entrances and exits of the chambers, huge steel gates were built. The gates were like double doors which opened and shut by parting in the middle. They were built so that they were hollow on the inside, which saved weight and made them light enough to open and close easily.

55. The construction of the locks began in August 1909, and it took a workforce of 48,000 men four years to complete the project. They had to mix five million bags of cement with sand and gravel to make enough concrete to build the locks' twelve massive chambers.

A finished lock

Completion

56. In October 1913, dynamite was exploded for the last time at the Culebra Cut. Two thousand miles (3,220 km) away at the White House in Washington, President Woodrow Wilson pressed a button, causing an explosion which saw water pouring into the Culebra Cut. After spending nine years and more than $350 million (around $8 billion in today's money), the United States had succeeded in building a fifty-one-mile-long (82 km) waterway connecting the Atlantic and Pacific Oceans.

57. On January 17, 1914, a boat that the French had abandoned years earlier, the *Alexandre La Valley*, was sent through the canal on a test run. The locks all worked perfectly and the test was a great success.

58. Back in the United States, there was great excitement at the completion of the canal, and huge celebrations were planned for the official opening on August 15. One hundred US warships would sail from Washington to Panama, before passing through the canal and sailing up the west coast of America to San Francisco.

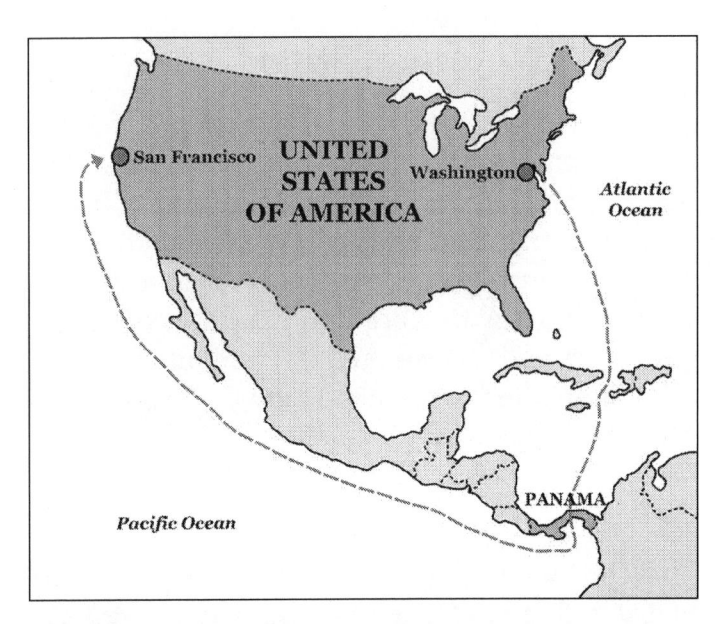

59. But the celebrations never happened. A few days before opening day World War One broke out when Germany declared war on France and Russia. Attention was now focussed on Europe, and instead of a procession of one hundred naval ships, an old cargo ship called *SS Ancon* became the first ship to travel across Panama once the canal was officially opened.

The SS Ancon passes through the canal

60. For more than one hundred years the Panama Canal has been an important shipping waterway, and nowadays around 14,000 ships use the canal every year. It earns money by charging every ship a toll, an amount which varies according to the ship's size and type of cargo.

61. Many people of Panama came to resent the fact that the United States controlled so much of their country, and relations between the two countries were often tense. In 1977, the US president, Jimmy Carter, and Omar Torrijos of Panama signed a treaty which agreed to hand over control of the canal to the Panamanians, and since December 31, 1999, the canal has been owned and operated by Panama.

Jimmy Carter and Omar Torrijos shake hands after signing the treaty

Assorted Panama Canal Facts

62. The United States came close to building the canal in Nicaragua, which had many advantages over Panama. Nicaragua is hundreds of miles closer to America than Panama, and there is a large lake and wide rivers that could have been used as part of the waterway. But a canal in Nicaragua would have been longer, and so it would have cost more and taken more time to build. In the summer of 1902, the US Senate voted in favor of Panama by 42 votes to 34.

63. When President Roosevelt sent warships to Panama to help the Panamanians in their rebellion against Colombia, many people across the world were outraged, accusing the president of bullying and acting illegally. But the president thought he was doing the right thing and eventually the outcry died down. With Panama breaking away from Colombian control, Roosevelt was able to get on with the construction of what he believed was "a great work for civilization."

64. More than 30,000 tons (27 million kg) of dynamite was used in the construction of the Panama Canal. Holes up to twenty-seven feet (8 m) deep were drilled into the rock, where the dynamite was placed and detonated. Drilling took place at all hours of the day, but the dynamite crews did their work at night or during the lunch break when other workers weren't around.

65. In November 1906, President Roosevelt visited Panama to check on how work was going, becoming the first US president to leave America while in office. He spent three days at the Canal Zone eating the same food as the workers and giving morale-boosting speeches. He came away from Panama very satisfied with the progress being made.

President Roosevelt at the controls of a huge digging machine

66. The largest ships that use the Panama Canal can be charged tolls of hundreds of thousands of dollars. But shipping companies think that is a price worth paying to save the time and expense of a long trip around South America. The lowest toll ever charged was in 1928, when an adventurer called Richard Halliburton paid just thirty-six cents to swim the length of the canal.

Richard Halliburton

Illustration Attributions

Cover
thyngum / CC BY-SA
(https://creativecommons.org/licenses/by-sa/2.0)
(changes made)

Title page
W. M. Welch / US Navy / Public domain
{{PD-US}}

Vasco Nunez de Balboa
Ober, Frederick A. 1906 / Public domain
{{PD-US}}

Ferdinand de Lesseps
http://vmgnico.free.fr/photo_ferd.html / Public domain
{{PD-US}}

John Frank Stevens
Originally uploaded by Mr Curly (Transferred by Orlodrim) 5 February 2012 20:07:09(UTC) (Originally uploaded at 2005-09-30 06:59:05) / Public domain Photograph originally from Makers of the Panama Canal, compiled and edited by F.E. Jackson, 1911
{{PD-US}}

William Gorgas
Unknown author / Public domain
circa 1918
{{PD-US}}

George Washington Goethals
Clinedinst / Public domain 1907
{{PD-US}}

Working on the Culebra Cut in 1907
H.C. White Co. / Public domain 1907
{{PD-US}}

The finished Gatun Dam
Author DeVerm /
https://creativecommons.org/licenses/by-sa/3.0/deed.en
https://creativecommons.org/licenses/by-sa/3.0/legalcode
(changes made)

The locks under construction in 1910
Unknown author / Public domain 1910
{{PD-US}}

A finished lock
Stan Shebs / CC BY-SA
(https://creativecommons.org/licenses/by-sa/3.0)

The *SS Ancon* passes through the canal
Unknown author / Public domain August 15 1914

Jimmy Carter and Omar Torrijos shake hands after signing the treaty
White House photo / Public domain 1977

President Roosevelt at the controls of a huge digging machine
Unknown author / Public domain November 1906

Richard Halliburton
Unknown author / Public domain

Made in the USA
Monee, IL
17 February 2025